Helping Children See Jesus

ISBN: 978-1-64104-026-6

Disobedience
*Old Testament Volume 20:
1 Samuel Part 1*

Author: Arlene S. Piepgrass
Illustrator: Todd Tennant
Computer Graphic Artist: Kristen Hall
Page Layout: Morgan Melton, Patricia Pope

© 2019 Bible Visuals International
PO Box 153, Akron, PA 17501-0153
Phone: (717) 859-1131
www.biblevisuals.org

All rights reserved. No part of this publication may be reproduced, stored in a retrieval system or transmitted in any form by any means, electronic, mechanical, photocopy, recording or otherwise, without the prior permission of the publisher, except as provided by USA copyright law.

RELATED ITEMS

To access related items (such as activities, memory verse posters and translated texts) please visit our web store at www.biblevisuals.org and enter 2020 at the top right of the web page. You may need to reduce the zoom setting to get the search box.

FREE TEXT DOWNLOAD

To obtain a FREE printable copy of the English teaching text (PDF format) under Product Format, please scroll down and select Extra–PDF Teacher Text Download. Then under Language select English before clicking the ADD TO CART button to place in your shopping cart. Other languages are available at an additional cost from the Language menu. When checking out, use coupon code XTACSV17 at checkout and click on Apply Coupon to receive the discount on the English text.

Only fear the LORD, and serve Him in truth with all your heart: for consider how great things He hath done for you. 1 Samuel 12:24

Lesson 1
DISOBEDIENCE IN THE FAMILY

NOTE TO THE TEACHER

During the 100 years prior to the time of the book of First Samuel, the people of Israel repeatedly disobeyed God. Rather than worshiping Him, they served the false gods of the Canaanites. They did not obey the command of God to destroy the neighboring heathen nations. When the Israelites genuinely repented of their sin and asked God to forgive them, He heard their prayers. Each time He raised up a strong leader–called a judge–to rescue them from their enemies. The Bible book of Judges explains these facts of Israel's past.

First Samuel continues the history of the Israelite people. Samuel lived during the lifetime of Samson and succeeded him as judge of Israel. During this time the Israelites were harshly treated by their enemies, the Philistines.

These historic lessons from the Bible record the power of sin and the severe consequences to all when discipline is lacking. God's hatred *for* sin and His punishment *of* sin, is a warning for us today (1 Corinthians 10:11; Romans 15:4; 6:23).

Scripture to be studied: 1 Samuel 1:1-3:21

The *aim* of the lesson: To show that God disciplines disobedience in the family.

What your students should *know:* That because God is good, He teaches fathers to discipline their children.

What your students should *feel:* Thankful for parents who teach the severe consequences of sinning against God.

What your students should *do:*

Those still in the care of parents–obey their parents; submit to their discipline.

Those who are parents–be firm with their children so they will willingly obey God.

Lesson outline (for the teacher's and students' notebooks):

1. The failure of Eli in his family (1 Samuel 2:12-17, 22-25).
2. God rejects the family of Eli (1 Samuel 2:27-36).
3. The obedience of Elkanah and Hannah (1 Samuel 1:1-2:11, 18-21).
4. God chooses Samuel (1 Samuel 2:35-3:21).

The verse to be memorized:

Only fear the LORD, and serve Him in truth with all your heart: for consider how great things He hath done for you. (1 Samuel 12:24)

THE LESSON

1. THE FAILURE OF ELI IN HIS FAMILY
1 Samuel 2:12-17, 22-25

Eli was important–indeed, the most important man in the land of Israel. He was the High Priest, the one who talked to God for the people. He taught the people the commands of God. He explained the absolute importance of obeying the Lord. He led the Israelites in their worship of God.

The High Priest was the only one who could go into the Most Holy Place (the Holy of Holies) in the Tabernacle. And he could enter just one day a year–the Day of Atonement. On that day he took blood from an animal sacrifice to sprinkle on the Ark of the Covenant. When God saw the blood, He forgave the sins of the High Priest and all the Israelites. (See Leviticus 16.)

Eli had two sons, Hophni and Phinehas. Because Eli was the High Priest, his sons were priests. It was a holy honor to be chosen by God to serve Him in the Tabernacle. (See 1 Samuel 2:28; Exodus 28:1; Leviticus 8:1-30. Long before Eli lived, God had chosen Aaron's family to serve as priests. Eli was a descendant of Aaron.)

Although the priests could not go into the Most Holy Place, they were allowed to enter the Holy Place. They were the ones who offered to God the sacrifices which the people brought when they worshiped Him. It was a solemn privilege to serve the Lord as a priest.

Hundreds of years before this, God had given definite instructions about the kinds of offerings the people were to bring. He explained clearly how the priests should kill the animals and exactly how the sacrifices were to be burned. (See Leviticus 6:1-7:38.)

God said, "Part of each sacrifice belongs to the priests. It will be food for their families." (See Leviticus 7:34-35; 10:14.)

The Lord also said, "Before you give the priests their portions, you must burn the fat that covers the inward parts." (See Leviticus 3:4-5; 10:15.) "The priests must be consecrated (*set apart*) to Me. (See Leviticus 8:22-24.) They must be willing to listen to My voice, serve Me obediently, and walk in My way. They are My representatives to My people."

Eli knew all the commands God had given. Therefore, what was his responsibility as a father? (Let students respond. *Eli must teach God's commands to his sons.*)

What must Hophni and Phinehas do? (*They must listen to and respect their father's teaching; obey God.*)

If Hophni and Phinehas rebel, refuse to listen to their father, and fail to obey God, what must Eli do? (*He must discipline his sons.*)

The Bible does not tell us whether or not Eli faithfully taught his sons. But it does say what they did when they became priests.

Show Illustration #1

Whenever a man came to offer a sacrifice to God, Hophni and Phinehas sent out a servant with a large fork. He jabbed the fork into the cooking pot, saying, "All the meat that comes up on the fork is for the priests!"

The worshiper, eager to obey God, replied, "I shall give you that part of the meat which the Lord commanded."

"That is not enough meat," the servant said, taking much more than he should. "Not only that, my master would rather roast the meat then have it boiled. From now on, give it to me raw," the servant demanded.

"No, no! God commands us to burn the fat first. Then you can have what you want," the obedient worshiper insisted.

"You give it to us or we shall take it by force," the servant shouted.

- 18 -

The two priests, Hophni and Phinehas, ignoring the laws of God, made their own laws. They insisted that the people disobey God. In time the Israelites stopped bringing sacrifices.

Hophni and Phinehas should have been good, obedient examples of Godly living. Instead, they did much that was sinful and wicked. They even copied the heathen priests who served idols (1 Samuel 2:22-23)! They made the worship of the Lord God exactly like the heathen worship. In fact the Bible indicates that Eli, the High Priest, was also selfish and sinful. He was more interested in good food than in obeying God's commands. He ate the forbidden meat with his two sons (1 Samuel 2:29).

2. GOD REJECTS THE FAMILY OF ELI
1 Samuel 2:27-36

Everyone was talking about the evil ways of Hophni and Phinehas. What do you think Eli should have done? (Encourage student Discussion. *Eli should have dismissed them from the priesthood. This was the punishment they deserved.*)

Instead of disciplining his sons, Eli told them, "I am hearing bad reports about your conduct. Remember: God will punish you for disobeying Him."

Hophni and Phinehas shrugged their shoulders and turned from their father. They continued their wickedness, refusing to obey him.

Because Eli did not discipline his sons, the Lord sent a warning to him by a man of God.

Show Illustration #2

"Eli, the Lord has given me a message for you," the man began. "You honor your sons more than God by allowing them to disobey His commands. Because *you* have not disciplined your sons, God will. Because of their wickedness, Hophni and Phinehas will die on the same day. The Lord God will choose another family to be priests–men who are willing to obey Him."

Eli was deeply troubled when he received this message from God. He knew he had waited too long to discipline his sons.

3. THE OBEDIENCE OF ELKANAH AND HANNAH
1 Samuel 1:1-2:11, 18-21

Now let me tell you about another Israelite family. Elkanah was the husband. He was not an important man. But he loved God. Each year he went to the Tabernacle (at Shiloh) to offer sacrifices and worship the Lord. This is where Eli, the High Priest, and Hophni and Phinehas, the priests, served God.

Elkanah's wife, Hannah, went with him. Because she had no children, she was too sad to eat. All she did was cry.

Finally Hannah slipped away from the crowd and went alone to the Tabernacle. Crying, she prayed, "Dear Lord, if You will give me a son, I shall give him back to You to serve You all his life."

Eli, sitting at the entrance of the Tabernacle, saw how brokenhearted Hannah was. He told her, "May God give you what you ask for."

Hannah was delighted! She believed God was going to answer her prayer. She hurried to her husband and, smiling, began to eat.

Within a year, Hannah had a baby boy. She named him "Samuel," which means *asked of God*. Why do you suppose she chose this name? (Let students answer.)

Hannah never forgot her promise. Surely when she rocked baby Samuel, she sang to him songs about God. As he grew, she often told him about the Tabernacle at Shiloh. She explained that the Lord God is holy and He hates sin. She told him about the worshipers and the sacrifices which they offered to have their sins forgiven.

Hannah would have explained, "Samuel, you are a gift from God. Before you were born, I promised the Lord I would give you to Him. Soon you will have a special privilege. You will live at the Tabernacle where you can serve God. Think of it, Samuel, you, my little boy, will be the servant of the Most High God. What an honor! Your father and I love you dearly. We shall miss you more than you can know. But we shall come to see you every year. We shall pray for you each day. Never, never will we forget you."

Do you think it would he easy for Hannah to give her son to God? NO! She was exactly like every mother–she loved her boy dearly. But she also loved God. And she was determined to keep her promise to Him.

The day came when Hannah said, "Samuel, you are young, but old enough for me to keep my promise to the Lord. It is time for us to go to Shiloh to worship God. Your father will take a sacrifice to he offered to the Lord for our sins. And, Samuel, you are going to stay there. You will help Eli in the Tabernacle. He, the High Priest, will give you duties and teach you how to serve the Lord God."

Hannah packed Samuel's clothes in a little bundle. And the three started their long walk to Shiloh. There Elkanah and Hannah offered an animal sacrifice to the Lord.

Show Illustration #3

Then they presented Samuel to Eli. Hannah explained, "Samuel is yours to train for the service of the Lord. God gave the boy to me. Now I am keeping my promise and am giving him to you for God's work."

Having given her only son to the Lord, Hannah prayed an interesting prayer. She began, "My heart is full of joy in the Lord."

Did you hear that? Hannah gave joyfully to the God of heaven. Do you give to Him that way? She not only offered God the required animal sacrifice. She gave her only son. And she was able to sing a song of rejoicing. Do *you* give to the Lord joyfully? (See 2 Corinthians 9:7.)

Turning to Samuel, Hannah said, "Your father and I must go back home now. But we shall come to visit you next year. And, Samuel, I shall bring you a brand new coat each year. I love you, Samuel. I shall pray for you every day. I am honored that God has a special work for you to do. Remember: always obey Eli. Listen carefully to all he teaches you about the Lord and His commands."

Samuel watched his mother and father disappear down the dusty road. Then, alone, he worshiped God in the Tabernacle.

For years young Samuel served in the House of God. He was obedient to the Lord and to Eli. (Read aloud slowly 1 Samuel 2:21b and 26.)

Do you think the Lord was pleased with Hannah's tremendous sacrifice? Indeed He was! In time, He blessed her with three more sons and two daughters.

4. GOD CHOOSES SAMUEL
1 Samuel 2:35-3:21

One night when Samuel was about 12 years old, he was sleeping soundly in the Tabernacle. Suddenly a voice called, "Samuel, Samuel."

Jumping from his bed, he ran to Eli, saying, "Here I am. You called me."

"I did not call you, my son," Eli said tenderly. "Go back to bed."

Show Illustration #4

Three times this happened. Finally Eli realized the Lord God was calling Samuel. So he said, "Samuel, the next time you hear the voice, say, 'Speak, Lord, for Your servant is listening'." Think of it! The Lord wanted to speak to young Samuel!

The Lord did call again. Samuel answered, "Speak, for Your servant is listening."

God sadly told the lad, "The time has come for Me to punish Eli's family exactly as I warned him."

Do you remember what warning the man of God had given Eli? (Review 1 Samuel 2:29-36.)

Do you think it was easy for Samuel to tell Eli the next morning what the Lord had told him? No, it was not. But Samuel gave a complete report of God's message.

Soon, just as God had warned, Hophni and Phinehas were both killed in battle on the same day (1 Samuel 4:11-14). When Eli heard the news, he fell backward off his bench–and died (1 Samuel 4:18)! God hates disobedience.

In time, Samuel became the prophet of God. He grew. The Lord was with him. And the people listened to him.

In his childhood at home, Samuel had been a normal boy who sometimes needed, and received, discipline. Apparently Hophni and Phinehas did whatever they pleased. Which turned out best?

Were you ever punished by your parents? Did you thank them for loving you enough to discipline you? Did you realize they were doing you a favor when they disciplined you?

God orders parents to teach His Word to their children. (See Deuteronomy 6:6-7; Proverbs 4:1.) He commands them to correct and discipline their children. (See Proverbs 3:11-12.) For children to disobey their parents is sin. Because Eli was not strict, his sons did not obey him. So when they grew older they would not obey God. And God punished them with death.

> **NOTE TO THE TEACHER**
>
> Are your students still under the care of their parents? If so, close with an appeal for them to determine to be obedient. Some of them might want to ask the prayer help of classmates for particular situations.
>
> If your students are parents, stress the importance of firmness, kindness, and consistence in teaching their children to obey.
>
> All ages should pray for forgiveness in any area of disobedience.

Lesson 2
DISOBEDIENCE IN THE NATION (Part 1)

Scripture to be studied: 1 Samuel 4:1-7:17

The *aim* of the lesson: To show that God judged the nation of Israel for disobeying Him.

What your students should *know*: That God is more powerful than any idol.

What your students should *feel*: A desire for their country and community to turn from false gods and obey the living God.

What your Christian students should *do*: Establish a good testimony (at home, school, work) so others will want to come to the Lord Jesus.

Lesson outline (for the teacher's and students' notebooks):
1. The Israelites ignore God (1 Samuel 4:1-5).
2. The Israelites defeated by the Philistines (1 Samuel 4:6-22).
3. God's superior power over Dagon (1 Samuel 5:1-6:21).
4. God shows the Philistines His power (1 Samuel 7:1-17).

The verse to be memorized:
> *Only fear the LORD, and serve Him in truth with all your heart: for consider how great things He hath done for you.* (1 Samuel 12:24)

> **NOTE TO THE TEACHER**
>
> At the time of this lesson the Israelite people were living in disobedience to God. They had entered the land God had promised them. But they had not obeyed His command to destroy the Philistines. Too, the Israelites turned to worshiping the heathen idols. They ignored the true and living God. Consequently, they were weak spiritually and morally. And the Philistines were overpowering them. They should have repented, sought God's forgiveness, and obeyed Him. Instead, they tried to solve their own problems by themselves. Disaster and defeat resulted.
>
> Observe, please, that the early part of this lesson took place *before* the deaths of Eli and his sons.

THE LESSON

Did you ever decide to do something which you knew your parents (teacher, or employer) did not want you to do? What happened? (Let students give examples.)

Were your parents happy when you disobeyed them? Did you say "I am sorry"? Did your parents punish you? Did they *keep on* loving you?

In our lesson today we are going to learn what happened when the people of Israel disobeyed God. Some, like Samuel and his parents, wanted to please God. But most men and women ignored God and chose to go their own way.

1. THE ISRAELITES IGNORE GOD
1 Samuel 4:1-5

The Philistines were enemies of God's people, the Israelites. They worshiped false gods–idols made by their own hands. They had chariots and iron swords. They were determined to conquer the Israelites and make them their slaves.

When Eli was a very old man, the Philistine army prepared to attack the Israelite people. What should the Israelites have done when they heard this? (Let class answer.) They should have prayed, asking God what to do. Instead, they made their own decision and marched right out to fight the enemy.

One Israelite soldier fell dead. Then another . . . and another! Israeli soldiers stumbled over their dead comrades.

"What is happening to our army?" they wailed. "Why is God letting the Philistines crush us? We cannot overthrow the Philistines!" They, God's very own people, had to retreat.

Dismayed, the Israelite soldiers raced back to their tents. "We lost 4,000 men! Why did God let the Philistines defeat us?" they moaned. "What shall we do? We do not want to be their slaves. How can we conquer them?"

Who could answer these questions for them? (*God.*) What would you have advised them to do? (*Ask Eli to pray for them and seek the Lord's help.*)

But again they paid no attention to God. One leader suggested, "Let's go to the Tabernacle and get the Ark of God. We can take it into battle with us."

"Yes, yes!" everyone shouted enthusiastically. "If we take the Ark with us we shall surely win. When our ancestors carried the Ark with them, God overthrew their enemies. Surely He will do the same for us!"

Do you remember what the Ark was? It was a box made of wood, covered with gold. It was almost four feet (11/8 meters) long, a little over two feet (2/3 meter) wide, and a bit more than two feet (2/3 meter) high. The top part of the Ark, the Mercy Seat, was made of solid gold. The Mercy Seat covered the box. At each end of the Mercy Seat was a solid gold cherub. Their wings were stretched toward each other. The presence of the Lord God rested between the two cherubs. What a sacred place that was! Think of it–the glory of God Almighty was right there among the Israelites!

The Ark was kept in the Holy of Holies, the most sacred place of the Tabernacle. No one except the High Priest was ever allowed to enter there. And he could go in only once a year on the Day of Atonement.

Now the Israelites had decided to get this precious Ark out of the Most Holy Place. They would take it with them into battle! How dared they think of using the holy Ark of God as a magical object?

They were not afraid, nor did they trust God for His help. Instead they sent orders to the priests, Hophni and Phinehas, in Shiloh. "Bring the Ark! You will lead our army against the Philistines."

Show Illustration #5

So the two sons of Eli obeyed the soldiers–and disobeyed God.

When Hophni and Phinehas brought the Ark into the camp, the soldiers were overjoyed. "Let's get out there and fight!" they shouted. "Now we shall conquer those Philistines! God parted the Jordan River when the priests carried the Ark before the people. The walls of Jericho fell when they carried the Ark around the city. Now that we have the Ark with us, we shall destroy the Philistines!"

2. THE ISRAELITES DEFEATED BY THE PHILISTINES
1 Samuel 4:6-22

But the Israelites had forgotten something. *God* had not told them to take the Ark this time, as He had before. Now they were trusting in the Ark instead of God.

The Philistines heard the shouting and cheering. "What is going on over in the Israelite camp?" they questioned.

Learning that the Israelites had the sacred Ark in their camp, the Philistines were terrified! "Now we do not have a chance!" they groaned. "Remember how their God defeated the Egyptians? Remember how they defeated those who lived here in this land? What shall we do? Oh, what shall we do?"

Their leaders shouted, "We must win this battle! If we lose, we shall be their slaves. Go! Fight with all your might!"

The Philistines raced toward the Israelites. The battle waged furiously. "Capture the Ark!" the Philistines shouted. "Israel will surrender if we capture the Ark!"

Show Illustration #6

That is exactly what the Philistines did. They captured the Ark. They killed Hophni, Phinehas and 30,000 Israelite soldiers.

Later when Eli heard that his sons were dead, he fell back off his bench, broke his neck and died. All this took place in one day! Do you remember the warning God had given Samuel? (Review previous lesson.) God means what He says. And what He says will happen, does happen. The Israelites were experiencing the dreadful price of disobeying God! (See Deuteronomy 28:25.)

3. GOD'S SUPERIOR POWER OVER DAGON
1 Samuel 5:1-6:21

The Israelites crept home defeated and discouraged. But the triumphant Philistines returned to their cities shouting, "We won! We defeated the Israelites! We captured the Ark! Now we have their God to help us!"

Proudly they marched to their temple in the city of Ashdod. There they displayed their trophy, the Ark, alongside Dagon, their handmade god. Think of it! The holy, precious Ark of the true and living God, alongside an idol made by the hands of man. Dagon had the body of a fish and the hands and head of a human. How hideous it looked!

Show Illustration #7

When morning came the people hurried to see the Ark–and to worship Dagon. To their amazement, Dagon had toppled over and lay on its face before the Ark.

"How did this happen?" the people asked. "Let's put Dagon back where it belongs." The men hauled their god to its usual position.

Early the next morning the Philistines rushed to the temple. To their horror, Dagon was not where it belonged. It lay in a heap before the Ark, its head and palms cut off! The Lord God was clearly teaching that power and honor belong only to Him. (See Psalm 96:5-8.)

What does this tell us about the idol? (Encourage student response. *It had no life–no power to help itself. The holy God of heaven has all power*. A perfect example of Psalm 115:3-8. Help your students to understand the uselessness of worshiping idols made by men.)

Quickly the triumph of the Philistines turned to disaster. Those living in and around the temple city (Ashdod) were tormented with horrid, painful boils. And mice were everywhere. (See 1 Samuel 6:4-5.)

"Where are all these mice coming from?" the people wailed. "They are ruining our fields! What shall we do?"

The men decided, "We cannot keep the Ark of God here. The God of Israel is against us and against Dagon, our god." Finally they agreed, "We shall take the Ark to the city of Gath."

When the Ark arrived in Gath, the men, young and old, immediately broke out with painful boils. So the people of Gath sent the Ark to another city, Ekron.

In Ekron, many immediately died when the Ark of God arrived. The men who lived were in agony with boils. They cried, "Send the Ark to Israel before we all die."

The Philistines should have realized that the God of Israel is the living God. If they had truly turned to Him they would have become part of God's family. Instead, they wanted to get rid of Him. They chose to continue worshiping the god they themselves had made.

Finally the Philistines made a wagon and sent the Ark of God to Israel. How glad the Israelites were to see it coming home!

4. GOD SHOWS THE PHILISTINES HIS POWER
1 Samuel 7:1-17

With the Ark returned, would the Israelites thank God? Would they tell Him they were sorry for having ignored Him? (Discuss.) I'm sorry to say they didn't.

They should have placed the Ark of God in the Tabernacle. Instead, they took it to someone's (Abinadab's) home. They selected another man (Ahinadab's son, Eleazar) to be in charge of it. But then they apparently forgot the Ark. And, like the nations around them, they worshiped false gods and idols. Year after year went by. They were not happy. Idols can never help or satisfy people because they are only man-made.

Twenty long years went by. The Philistines continued to trouble the people of Israel. What advice would you have given the Israelites? (Discuss.)

"I think the Lord our God has forgotten us," the people of Israel were saying to each other. Was this true? NO! *They* had forgotten God!

Samuel heard what they were saying. "Are you serious about wanting to return to the Lord God?" he asked.

"Yes, yes!" the people exclaimed.

Samuel began, "If you really want to turn to the Lord, destroy all your false gods. Determine to obey only the living God and worship Him alone. Tell God you are sorry for your sins. Then come together at Mizpah and I shall pray for you."

The Israelites went home and destroyed all their idols. They really wanted God to forgive them. They wanted to worship and obey Him. Do you think God forgave them? Remember: they had disobeyed Him for many years.

Long before, God had made a wonderful promise to the Israelites. "If you are truly sorry for your sins and confess them to Me," He said, "I shall forgive you." (See Deuteronomy 30:1-3; Isaiah 1:18-19.)

The people gathered with Samuel at Mizpah. They did not eat all day. "We've sinned against You, our God," they confessed.

Suddenly someone shouted, "The Philistines are coming! The Philistines are coming!"

"Oh, Samuel, pray for us," the Israelites begged. "We'll be destroyed if God doesn't help us. We're not prepared to fight."

Show Illustration #8

Samuel immediately offered a baby lamb as a sacrifice. Then he prayed. And God saw that His people were genuinely sorry for their sins. He is a loving God who hears and answers prayer. (See 1 John 5:14-15.) Do you think the Lord answered? (Let students give ideas.)

The Philistine general urged his men onward. Certain of victory, he doubtless shouted, "We shall destroy the Israelites completely! Look! They are not even trying to fight!"

Right then something most unusual happened. (*Teacher:* Read 1 Samuel 7:10 slowly.)

The Lord thundered mightily. The Philistines were terrified and ran away. The Israelites chased them and struck them down. (See 1 Samuel 7:11-13. Read verse 13 slowly.)

What lesson should Israel have learned that day? (Allow discussion.)

Samuel set up a stone as a landmark of what happened there. He reminded the people so all could hear, "The Lord has helped us!"

What have you learned for yourself from our lesson? (Suggest personal applications from the lesson.)

1. God hates disobedience.
2. The consequences of disobeying God are defeat, distress, heartache.
3. The living God is all-powerful over false gods.
4. Idols have no power to help people.
5. Men are powerless before the living God.
6. When we confess our sins, God is faithful and just to forgive our sins. (1 John 1:9.)

If you have not already done so, will you decide today to trust in the living God? (Review Steps of Salvation given on page 8.)

Lesson 3
DISOBEDIENCE IN THE NATION

Scripture to be studied: 1 Samuel 8-12

The *aim* of the lesson: To show that God sometimes allows His people to have their own way even though it is not His perfect plan for them.

What your students should *know*: That what everyone else is doing is not always right for us to do.

What your students should *feel*: A desire for God's best for their lives.

What your students should *do*: Decide what they can do this week in obedience to God, thus doing His perfect will.

Lesson outline (for the teacher's and students' notebooks):

1. The Israelites demand a king (1 Samuel 8).
2. God chooses Saul (1 Samuel 9-10).
3. Saul defeats the Ammonites (1 Samuel 11).
4. Samuel warns the Israelites (1 Samuel 12).

The verse to be memorized:

Only fear the LORD, and serve Him in truth with all your heart: for consider how great things He hath done for you. (1 Samuel 12:24)

NOTE TO THE TEACHER

God may let us have our own way even though it is not His choice for us. Obedience honors God. Disobedience brings sorrow to ourselves! The living Lord of the Israelites–by His power alone–had defeated the Philistines. God's people should have been satisfied with his leadership. But now they wanted a king so they could be like the other nations around them. How foolish! What human king could do the great things God had done for them? It is important that we continually remember what the Lord God had done for us, and give praise and thanks to Him!

THE LESSON

"Everybody is doing it!" Have you ever said that?

Is it always good and right to be like everybody else?

The Israelites wanted to be like everybody else. Let's see what happened.

1. THE ISRAELITES DEMAND A KING
1 Samuel 8

Once, a group of Israelite men gathered secretly. Listen to what they doubtless said.

"Samuel is getting old," the head man remarked, "He has led us well. But now he has set his sons over us as judges (leaders). They are not like their father. They are not honest as he has been. They take bribes from people. They make unfair decisions."

Show Illustration #9

He added, "I think we should have a king to reign over us–like the other nations around us!"

"A king?" all the men gasped. After a long silence, one decided, "Maybe that is a good idea! All the surrounding nations have kings. I think we should tell Samuel we want a king!"

An older man spoke quietly: "Men, do you realize what you're saying? We don't need a king. God is our King. He alone reigns over us. Remember how He defeated our enemies, the Philistines? (See 1 Samuel 7.) Before that He led our ancestors out of Egypt. (Briefly review the crossing of the Red Sea, Exodus 14.) Don't forget what God has done. He led us into this land and conquered all the kings who lived here. We do not need a king. Our king, the Lord God, is all-powerful."

But the others refused to listen. They wanted a king *like everybody else*. Finally they persuaded the elders to go to Samuel. They told him, "You are old, Samuel. And your sons do not lead us in the right way. We want a king like all the other nations."

How do you think Samuel felt? (*Displeased, sad.*) He did not give them an answer immediately. He was greatly troubled. He had tried to be a good leader. Now the people of Israel were rejecting him. So he prayed to the Lord.

God comforted him, saying, "Samuel, the people have not rejected you. They have rejected *Me* as their King. They are ignoring all *I* have done for them. If they insist on having a king, they will have all kinds of trouble." God explained exactly what would come to His people if they had a king. Then he added, "If My people must have their own way, they can expect severe consequences."

Samuel returned to the leaders with God's message: "God has told me to warn you what a king will do. He will send your sons to war. Your daughters will become servants of the king. He will take your best crops for his use. He will take your choice animals for himself. You will pay high taxes. You yourselves will become the king's servants. Then you will beg God to help you. But He will not answer you!"

"We want a king!" the people insisted. "We want to be like all the other nations around us!" The Israelites wanted their own way. They refused to listen to the Lord God of heaven. Think of that!

God told Samuel, "I do not want the people of Israel to have a king. Even so, I shall choose one for them."

2. GOD CHOOSES SAUL
1 Samuel 9-10

A few days later, God told Samuel a secret. "About this time tomorrow I am going to send a young man to you. He will be looking for his father's donkeys. He is the one I have chosen to be king. Pour oil on his head. Tell him he will be the king of My people, the Israelites."

The very next day, a young man, named Saul, and his servant came to Samuel. They were looking for their lost donkeys. But they did not tell Samuel this.

The young, good-looking Saul did not know God's secret. So he was amazed when Samuel said, "Do not worry about your lost donkeys. They have been found."

Samuel continued, "Come and have dinner with my guests and me. Tomorrow I shall tell you some great things which are in store for you."

Great things for me? Saul wondered. *What is he talking about?*

Saul followed Samuel into the banquet hall. There he had another surprise. He, Saul, was given a seat of honor at the head table. He was even more puzzled when the servants gave him the best piece of meat to eat.

– 23 –

Early the next morning Samuel started with Saul and his servant on their journey. Samuel told Saul, "Ask your servant to go ahead. I have a message for you from God."

Show Illustration #10

When they were alone, Samuel poured olive oil on Saul's head. "God has chosen you to be king of the Israelites," Samuel announced.

Me? King of Israel? thought Saul. *I am only a farm boy. My family is not important. I cannot be king.*

The Bible tells us that as Saul turned toward home, God changed his heart. (1 Samuel 10:9.) He knew then that the Lord would give him all the ability he would need. He was ready to lead and rule the people of Israel.

When Saul got home he did not tell anyone what happened.

Later Samuel called the Israelites together. He reminded them, "You have refused to have God as your King. You want to be like all the other nations. So you shall have an earthly ruler. Now I want you to meet the man who will soon become your king."

But the man could not be found. He was hiding.

"Where is he?" everyone asked.

God was the only One who knew where the king-elect was. He told Samuel where the man was hiding.

So the men found him and brought him out. Samuel announced, "Here is Saul, the man God has chosen to be your king some day." Saul stood taller and more handsome than anyone else. (See I Samuel 9:2; 10:23.)

The people were delighted. "Long live the king!" they shouted. Soon they would be like all the other nations.

Samuel had some advice for the Israelites and for Saul. "You want a king so you will be like other nations," he began. "But any king you have must be *different* from the kings of other nations. Your king always will have to he chosen by the Lord God, not by the people." (See Deuteronomy 17:15.) Everyone nodded in agreement.

"Your king must be an Israelite, never a foreigner." The people understood.

"Your king dare not become extravagant. He must not make himself rich with horses, gold, or silver. (See Deuteronomy 17:16-17.) Above all, he is required to have his own copy of God's law. He must study it, obey it, and fear the Lord God. God is His ruler and he must be subject to Him." (See Deuteronomy 17:18-20.)

Most Israelites were delighted that Saul would be their king some day. But there were troublemakers who despised him.

3. SAUL DEFEATS THE AMMONITES
1 Samuel 11

After the meeting, everyone returned home. Life went on as usual. Saul went back to farming.

One day, Saul came from the fields with his oxen, and heard the villagers crying loudly. "What's the matter?" he asked.

"Our enemies, the Ammonites, have attacked the Israelites who live in Jabesh-Gilead."

The messengers from Jabesh-Gilead who had brought this bad news added, "We do not want to fight. We asked the Ammonites to make peace with us. They agreed, but only if we let them gouge out the right eye of every Israelite in the city."

Saul was furious. "The Ammonites want to make our soldiers useless. With a man's left eye behind his shield and his right eye gone, he could not see to fight. NO! You Israelites will *not* lose your right eyes. We shall fight!"

Now Saul would need an army. Would the men of Israel go to battle at his command?

Show Illustration #11

Saul sent messengers throughout the land of Israel. Everywhere they showed pieces of oxen which Saul had cut up. One announced, "This is Saul's message: 'If you refuse to join our army, Your oxen will be killed and cut into pieces like these'." Hearing this, the terror of the Lord fell on the Israelites. And 333,000 men turned out to fight.

Early the next morning, Saul and his army made a surprise attack. They broke into the enemy camp and totally defeated the Ammonites!

The Israelites were delighted with what Saul had done. "Long live the king!" they shouted. "Long live the king! He has led us to victory over our enemies. We will kill anyone who is against Saul!"

"No one will be killed!" Saul exclaimed. "I didn't win the victory. The Lord rescued us from our enemies!"

Then Samuel told the people, "Come! We shall go to Gilgal. There in the presence of the Lord we shall declare that Saul is our king." So they all went and enjoyed a great celebration. Do you think the Israelites were right in choosing Saul?

(*Teacher:* Lead discussion. It *seems* as if they were. But is it ever right to reject what God wills? Read Isaiah 40:21-24, 28-31. Emphasize the omnipotence–all-powerfulness–of God. By contrast, read Isaiah 40:6-8, which speaks of all humans, including Saul. Would God or Saul be the better king?)

4. SAMUEL WARNS THE ISRAELITES
1 Samuel 12

Samuel was now an old man. He knew it was time to give up his work as judge of the Israelites. He had served God faithfully as their leader for many years. He would continue his work of priest and prophet. From now on Saul would be their king and leader.

Samuel called together the people of Israel. "You have chosen a king to rule over you," he said. "But do not forget the Lord your God. Every time our ancestors failed to obey His commands, He punished them. If you disobey the Lord, and if you rebel against Him, He will punish you. But if you honor the Lord God, obey Him, and keep His commandments, He will bless you and your king." All the people agreed.

Show Illustration #12

But their smiles disappeared when Samuel continued: "You have been wicked in asking for a king. You know it does not rain at this time of year when you harvest wheat. But I am going to ask the Lord to send thunder and rain. Then you will know how evil it was for you to have asked for a king."

Then Samuel prayed to the Lord. And that same day God sent thunder and rain. Oh, how it rained! At once the Israelites realized that by demanding a king, they had sinned against God.

"Pray for us, Samuel," they begged. "If you do not pray for us, we shall die!"

"God still loves you," Samuel reassured the people. "He will not leave you. You are His special people whom He has chosen for Himself. But remember, no useless idols can help you. Our God in heaven is the living and powerful One who hears and answers prayers. Remember Him. Serve Him with all your heart. Obey all His commands. Do not be afraid." (Read 1 Samuel 12:24-25.)

What a gracious and forgiving God the Israelites served! And He is *our* God–the One we serve today. Let us repeat together our memory verse. (1 Samuel 12:24.)

Samuel had reminded the Israelites that God previously led them out of slavery in Egypt. He protected them and gave them victory over their enemies. (*Teacher:* Read Romans 8:32 slowly to your class.) What has God done for us? (*He gave His only Son to die on the cross for us who are slaves of sin*.) Have you ever accepted God's great gift of salvation? Is the Lord Jesus Christ King of your life?

Since God has done so much for you, what is your responsibility to Him? (*"Serve Him in truth with all your heart."*) How can you serve Him? (Let students discuss what they can do for the Lord today and in the week to come. Each should write his decision in his notebook.)

Lesson 4
DISOBEDIENCE OF THE KING

NOTE TO THE TEACHER

Before introducing this lesson, give students an opportunity to report the joys they had in serving the Lord since the previous lesson.

To drift away from God is pitiful. Sin takes root and the life gradually changes. The person who goes his own way instead of God's way, goes deeper and deeper into sin. His end is destruction (Proverbs 16:25). Saul knew what God commanded him to do. Yet gradually his heart became cold toward the Lord. One sin led to another. Doing wrong became easy. He was interested only in himself. As he departed from God, he fled faster and faster down the broad road to destruction. So it will be with anyone who chooses his own way.

Scripture to be studied: 1 Samuel 13:1-15:35

The *aim* of the lesson: To show that disobedience and self-will can lead to tragedy, misery, and rejection.

  What your students should *know*: God sees all we do; no sin is hidden from Him.

  What your students should *feel*: A desire to be honest always in every situation.

  What your students should *do*: Always tell the truth; obey authority; honor the Lord with their lips and their lives.

Lesson outline (for the teacher's and students' notebooks):
1. The impatience of King Saul (1 Samuel 13:1-23).
2. The foolish leadership of Saul (1 Samuel 14:1-52).
3. The partial obedience of Saul (1 Samuel 15:1-21).
4. God rejects King Saul (1 Samuel 15:22-35).

The verse to be memorized:

Only fear the LORD, and serve Him in truth with all your heart: for consider how great things He hath done for you. (1 Samuel 12:24)

THE LESSON

Obedience is one of the hardest lessons for us to learn. We all like to have our own way. But remember: We may choose to disobey God, but we cannot change the consequences of what we have chosen! (Review briefly the experience of Adam and Eve in the garden.)

1. THE IMPATIENCE OF KING SAUL
1 Samuel 13:1-23

Things were going badly for the people of Israel. The Israelites knew the Philistines were again gathering their huge army. They had 3,000 chariots, 6,000 horsemen, and more soldiers than could be counted.

King Saul was worried. He had chosen only 3,000 soldiers (1 Samuel 13:2). How could he ever defeat the Philistines with such a small army?

Who could give the king ability to win? (*God.*) Earlier, Samuel had told King Saul to go to Gilgal. "Wait there seven days for me, Saul," he commanded. "I shall meet you at Gilgal. After I offer sacrifices to God, I shall tell you what to do." (See 1 Samuel 10:8.)

So Saul the king waited. But the Philistines were moving closer. Their army grew in number. Saul's soldiers were frightened. They hid in caves, in cliffs, in pits. Some moaned, "We shall never be able to defeat the Philistines. We do not have any chariots, or swords, or spears. (1 Samuel 13:19-21.) How can we ever overcome them? We shall be destroyed!"

Consequently Saul's army had fewer men than before. Those who did remain trembled with fear. One asked, "Why doesn't King Saul lead us into battle? What is he waiting for?"

Saul should have encouraged his soldiers by reviewing what God had done for them at Jabesh-Gilead. (Have students tell incident from Lesson 3, I Samuel 11.) Saul could have reminded himself that God had won the victory. He ought to have remembered the thunderstorm God sent to show that their request for a king had displeased Him. He should have assured his soldiers that Samuel would be coming to tell them what to do.

Instead, Saul paced back and forth before his tent. He thought, *This is the seventh day. Samuel is not yet here. My soldiers are deserting me. What shall I do?*

A leader asked, "How much longer are we going to wait, King Saul? Our men are leaving. You cannot fight the Philistines without an army."

"You are right!" answered Saul. "But we cannot fight until we offer a sacrifice to God. Since Samuel has not come, bring the animals to me."

Show Illustration #13

Saul then prepared the offering, burnt it, and prayed. "Now we shall fight," he announced. "We cannot wait any longer."

Did King Saul do what was right? (Let students discuss. *Saul was wilfully disobeying God. Only the priest was to offer sacrifices. Samuel, God's priest, had said "Wait."*) Instead of waiting, Saul did what he wanted to do.

At that moment, Samuel arrived. Seeing the burning sacrifice, he asked, "Saul, what have you done?" (Have students read 1 Samuel 13:11-12.)

Saul answered, "You really cannot blame me for what I did. What else could I have done?" Was he telling the truth? Do you think God would have forgiven Saul if he had confessed his sin and prayed for forgiveness? (*Absolutely.* Examples: 1 Samuel 7:2-10; 12:19-25.)

Saul was too proud to ask God to forgive him. Samuel told him sadly, "Saul, you have been very foolish. You know that only a priest is to offer sacrifices. You have disobeyed the Lord God. God had planned for your sons to rule the people of Israel after you. But because you disobeyed Him, He has now chosen someone else to be king."

Samuel turned then and disappeared.

2. THE FOOLISH LEADERSHIP OF SAUL
1 Samuel 14:1-52

King Saul sadly retreated with only 600 men. He was discouraged. He was afraid. What a poor leader!

One of Saul's soldiers was his own son, Jonathan. He was different from his father. He trusted the Lord God. He was brave. He asked God for guidance.

One day Jonathan had an idea. He turned to the young man who carried his armor. "Some of the Philistines are camped across the ravine on that high cliff," Jonathan whispered. "Come! You and I shall go over and attack them. The Lord God does not need a big army to defeat our enemies. He can do it just as easily with two!"

"I am ready to do whatever you say, Jonathan," the armor-bearer replied.

"We want to be sure this is God's will," Jonathan cautioned. (*Teacher:* Read aloud 1 Samuel 14:8-10.)

The Philistines saw Jonathan and his armor-bearer crossing over toward them. "Come up here!" they shouted.

Jonathan whispered to his armor-bearer, "Follow me! The Lord has handed the Philistines over to Israel." The two climbed to the top of the army post and quickly killed 20 men. Then the earth shook. The Philistines were terrified!

King Saul's lookouts were watching from afar. When they saw the Philistines melting away in all directions, they reported to the king. Saul shouted, "Who is attacking them? Who is missing from our camp?"

"Jonathan and his armor-bearer aren't here!" came the reply. Quickly Saul gathered his men to join in the battle.

"Listen to me!" Saul commanded. "Anyone who eats anything today will be cursed. Eat absolutely nothing until I gain the victory over our enemies."

Why should Saul give such a foolish command? (*He wanted to be credited with defeating the Philistines. He wanted others to see that he, the king, was in control.*)

Jonathan had not heard his father's command. As he chased the Philistines through the forest, he saw some honey. He dipped a stick into the honeycomb and licked the honey. Immediately he was refreshed and continued fighting.

But the other soldiers were famished. They became so weak they could not defeat the Philistines.

Later Jonathan heard about his father's foolish command. He told the soldiers, "No wonder you did not have strength enough to fight. If only you had taken some honey we could have had a great victory today. My father has caused trouble."

Saul was furious when he learned that Jonathan had disobeyed his command.

"Jonathan, my son, you shall die!" he vowed.

Show Illustration #14

"No, he will not die!" shouted the soldiers. "He is the one God used to win the victory today. Not one hair on his head will fall to the ground!" Quickly the men rescued Jonathan.

The same people who had insisted on having a king, were now opposing him. Saul was humiliated before his army. Why? Because he chose to do what he wanted rather than asking God for guidance.

The Lord had warned the people that their king would become a dictator. (See 1 Samuel 8:9-18.) And this was just the beginning.

3. THE PARTIAL OBEDIENCE OF SAUL
1 Samuel 15:1-21

One day Samuel came to Saul with a message from God. "Listen carefully," he said. "The Amalekites are wicked. Back when our people were marching toward Canaan, the Amalekites made a cowardly attack on the old men, women, and children who brought up the rear. (See Deuteronomy 25:17-19; Exodus 17:1-16.) God said we should punish them when we got in the land. His command should have been obeyed long ago. Now, King Saul, lead your army against the Amalekites. Destroy all of them–their king, the men, the women, and children. And, Saul, get rid of all the animals. Do not spare *anything*!"

Was God's command clear? (*Yes*! Remind students of God's promise in Genesis 12:3. The Amalekites had cursed Israel.)

Obeying the command of God, Saul assembled his army. "Attack!" he shouted. Quickly he and his soldiers totally defeated the Amalekites.

Show Illustration #15

The men examined the sheep and all the other animals. One soldier asked, "King Saul, do you really think we should kill all of them? Could we keep some of the best ones?"

What should Saul answer? (Let students respond.)

He should have shouted, "NO!" Instead he replied, "I guess it'll be all right to spare the best animals. But kill the rest!"

What is wrong with his answer? (*He disobeyed God's command.*)

"Have all the people been killed?" Saul asked the soldiers.

"Yes, every one of them, except the king whom you have captured. Do you want us to kill him now?" the soldiers asked.

"No," replied Saul.

What was wrong with Saul's decision? (*He wilfully disobeyed God*.)

Saul was so elated with his victory that he built a monument to honor himself (1 Samuel 15:12). But even though Saul was proud of himself, who was angry with him? (*God*. 1 Samuel 18:11.)

God told Samuel, "I am sorry Saul refused to obey Me. I can no longer use him as king over My people."

When Samuel went to Saul, Saul greeted him cheerfully. "Samuel, I have obeyed the command of the Lord."

Samuel replied, "I hear the sounds of bleating sheep and lowing cattle. What does this mean?"

Saul replied, "The soldiers saved the best animals. We're going to sacrifice them to the Lord your God. But we destroyed everything else."

4. GOD REJECTS KING SAUL
1 Samuel 15:22-35

Sadly, Samuel said, "Why did you disobey the Lord God, Saul? Why did you rebel against Him and do evil in His sight? God does not want your sacrifices. He wants obedience! Because you have rejected the word of the Lord, Saul, He has rejected you as king of the Israelites."

Saul was shocked. "I have sinned. I have listened to the people instead of God. Please forgive me and go worship the Lord with me."

"No, indeed, Saul," Samuel said firmly. "I shall not go with you. Because you disobeyed God, He has rejected you as king over Israel!"

Saul was desperate. Grabbing Samuel to keep him from leaving, Saul tore Samuel's robe.

Show Illustration #16

Turning to Saul, Samuel said, "Just as you have torn my robe, so God has torn from you the Kingdom of Israel. He has given it to another who is better than you. This is final. God means what He says."

Saul was frantic. "Please, please forgive me," he begged. "I have sinned. But come and worship with me and honor me before the people."

Samuel did go with Saul. "Bring King Agag to me," Samuel demanded. "I shall show you how much God despised the evil of that wicked king." Samuel killed Agag as King Saul watched, horrified.

Saul's life continued downward. When he committed sin and was charged with it, he excused himself. So Saul became more wicked and miserable until the day he died.

If the story of *your* life were to be told, what would be said of you? Have you, like Saul, refused to obey God and His Word? Listen carefully to what the Lord says.

Teacher: Close solemnly by reading Scripture verses which are applicable to your group. For example, if you are teaching *children*, you could use Ephesians 6:1-3; Colossians 3:20.

Young People: 1 Peter 5:5; 1 Timothy 4:12.
Wives: Ephesians 5:22-24; 1 Peter 3:1-6.
Husbands: Ephesians 5:25, 28; 1 Peter 3:7.
Employees: Ephesians 6:5-8; Colossians 3:22-25; 1 Timothy 6:1; 1 Peter 2:18-20.
Employers: Colossians 4:1.
Unsaved: 2 Thessalonians 1:7-9, 1 Peter 4:17.
All believers: Hebrews 13:17.

These are serious commands of the Lord God to be obeyed. Remember: Those who disobey God and His Word must suffer the consequences. For God always disciplines those who sin.

www.ingramcontent.com/pod-product-compliance
Lightning Source LLC
Chambersburg PA
CBHW060803090426
42736CB00002B/142